Quality Time
and Other Quandaries

Thank you to Peter Sussman, Stuart Dodds,
and especially to Donald Brown.

Copyright © 1992 by Chronicle Publishing Company. All rights reserved.
No part of this book may be reproduced in any form without written
permission from the publisher.

Printed in the United States of America.
ISBN 0-8118-0035-0
Library of Congress Cataloging in Publication Data available.

Cover design: Bradley Crouch
Book design: Christine Kristen
Distributed in Canada by Raincoast Books,
112 East Third Avenue, Vancouver, B.C. V5T 1C8

10 9 8 7 6 5 4 3 2 1

Chronicle Books
275 Fifth Street
San Francisco, CA 94103

Quality Time
and Other Quandaries

New Cartoons by Gail Machlis

Chronicle Books   San Francisco

"*Don't think for a moment that you're leaving without these lamps.*"

"Don't think for a moment that you're leaving without
these lamps."

*"James, you need to stop playing with your food or
leave the table."*

"You make me feel insignificant. You treat me like a child. You belittle me, You don't like my friends, you get angry with me when I see them, you don't want me to succeed, you undermine me, nothing I say is correct, I can't even choose a movie or order DINNER, you think the things I'm interested in are ridiculous, everything is rational and calculated to you, you're not supportive of my work, you don't want to take me seriously, you want to own me and control everything, but people aren't like -- you can't run their lives or derive your security from possessing them. You can't expect me to spend my life trying to be what you think I should be."

BUT I _LOVE_ YOU.

machlis

Well then go if you have to. A therapist is just going to tell you the exact same things I've been telling you for years.
machlis

Do you ever think about people who live in those places off Highway 5-- like Butterworth, California? You know, the motel owners who never go home, never see anything that is actually growing -- I mean really, if you consider the Quality... I know we all make choices, but can you imagine?
I thought we were going to fool around tonight.
machlis

"Well, yes, given a choice, I suppose I do prefer to write
a bad review."

All year long we pay double
for organic vegetables
and now you're
going to use insect
repellent.

Invited to dinner at the Spragues, Mrs. Beamer rudely
asks if they might watch another channel.

Visit to Mom

Dog Obedience Videos

"You know I was talking with my aerobics instructor after class, and she was saying how it doesn't seem like you and I have that much in common anymore."

"...and you mocked me when I played Ba
in the womb."

"You get the Spragues and Fords on weekends, she gets Bruce Emory and Bill and Faye Waters for holidays, you alternate summers for the Wongs and Robisons."

I knew right away
we'd have a lot in common.
She was wearing a Frieda
Kahlo T-shirt.

"There's no doubt in my mind. It's definitely a hole in the ozone layer."

You have to admit it's amazing. 2½, and reading the New York Times!
Yes, but he has no comprehension of foreign affairs.
machlis

Can you believe it? They've discovered a galaxy one billion miles away that has more than 100 trillion stars and is 60 times larger than the Milky Way.
probably no single men
machlis

"*Wait until she finds out we both sleep on the bed.*"

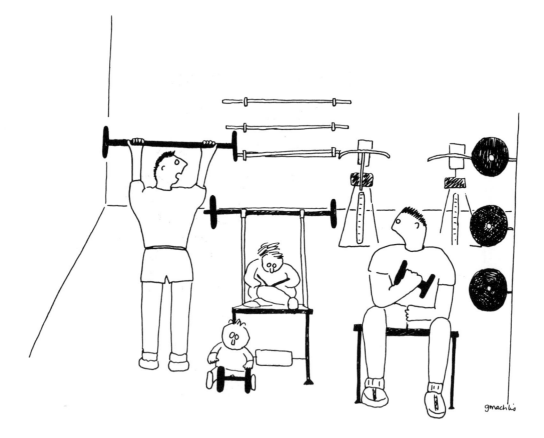

"I just felt like I wasn't spending enough time
with the kids."

Be prepared

"I wish you had told me it was subtitled. I really just felt like relaxing tonight."

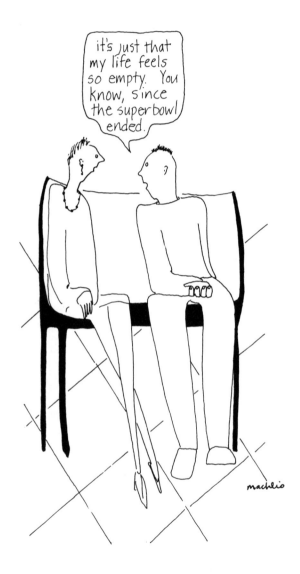

I'm distraught about Salman Rushdie and that WOODSTOCK-SKINHEAD thing! Not to MENTION the DROUGHT and the OZONE. I have nightmares about DIOXIN and then those book-stores being bombed! I'm short-tempered with my children, too.
I HAVE JUST THE PILL.
machlis

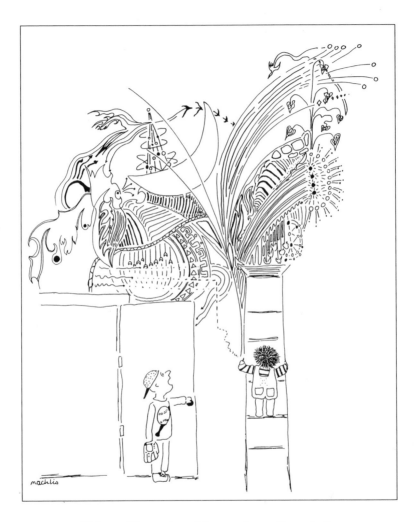

"Mom...Horace is writing on the walls again."

Spring Cleaning

"*What's really distressing is how little I must have thought of myself to buy an outfit like this.*"

"He's been like this all day. He's mourning his record collection. We should never have bought him the CD player."

Well, here, she's free a week from Friday for an hour before ballet. Perhaps they could play then.

"No need to worry. She's very good with delicate things."

"*So what did you put down for Question 15 — 'Have*
ever experienced rapture?'"

"As you can see, Mr. Bean, a transplant is our only
option. Top to bottom, you've got bad Karma."

We've found the most wonderful nursery school. Alice Waters' daughter went there.
machlis

"I see diapers, many, many diapers."

"I'd rather have mine microwaved."

ENTERING THE PARK

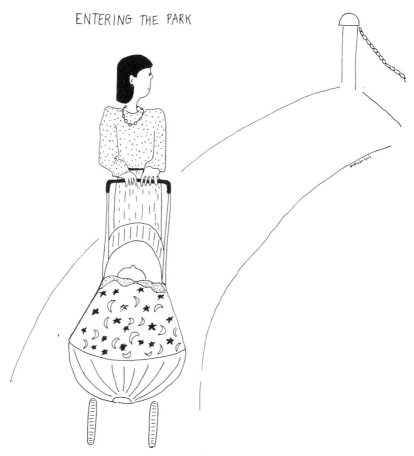

Assume a casual attitude, as if
you are somehow unaware that
your child is the most extra-
ordinary thing ever to set foot
on earth.